THE
FIRST
ECHO

THE
FIRST
ECHO

POEMS

SHANE SEELY

Louisiana State University Press

Baton Rouge

Published by Louisiana State University Press
Copyright © 2019 by Shane Seely
All rights reserved
Manufactured in the United States of America
LSU Press Paperback Original

Designer: Laura Roubique Gleason
Typefaces: Minion Pro text with Gotham display
Printer and binder: LSI

Lines from Michael Burkard, "Goodbye," from *Entire Dilemma* (1998), reproduced by permission of Sarabande Books.

Cataloging-in-Publication Data are available from the Library of Congress.

ISBN 978-0-8071-6963-6 (pbk.: alk. paper) — ISBN 978-0-8071-6965-0 (pdf) — ISBN 978-0-8071-6964-3 (epub)

The paper in this book meets the guidelines for permanence and durability of the Committee on Production Guidelines for Book Longevity of the Council on Library Resources. ∞

For Sonia and Maria,
my team all needed

Goodbye to your face, only so I can
say hello to your face.

—Michael Burkard

CONTENTS

WHAT YOU KNOW YOU CAN'T OUTRUN

GOD'S BLUE VOICE

Feeling Good Night and
She Is Love

Dear Paul, lately I have been half
in love with the old radio mystery plays
that beamed across the darkness
of the 1940s and into the homes
of our grandparents and across
the oceans into the tents and trenches
of soldiers, into the hospitals
where the wounded lay dying . . .
I love them, as the audience then
must have loved them in another time
of war, for their predictability—
if one man picks up a hitchhiker
on a rainy night and a report
of a murder comes across the car radio,
one of them did it. You don't know
at first which one is lying, but
both are, and one's a detective,
and the other will within the half hour
stumble into the open field of his guilt.
After they cut the first cancer
from your brain, you wrote
for everyone to read: *I am sure*
of it again. Thank you Lord! Feeling
good night and she is love. Angie
is my might halo. The wildest love!
And it was so beautiful we knew
you could not die. And Angie,
who salved the wounds
the staples made along your scalp—
you stood up again and married her,
and good for you, beside the ocean.
Of course you suspect at first
that the detective is the murderer—
he is grave and strange and his

shoes are thick with mud, and the driver
seems almost overwhelmed
by just the weather. But that's the trick
of it, the mouse of a man
who beats his spinster aunt to death
for money she doesn't have,
then beats it trembling for the coast. When
the cancer came back you called
on God again, said you felt Him strong
in you, though I'd like to think
that what you felt was, at long
last, love. But even that was not
enough to keep them from opening
your head again. You wrote
Angie has my team all needed. You wore
a t-shirt that said *I had brain surgery,
what's your excuse?* At the end
of every mystery, someone must
tell the story of what really happened,
because what makes it a mystery
is that we arrive too late to know.
The cancer killed you. Two men
got into a car and one of them died,
and the other was cancer. We know
the story well: sooner or later
the world is just two voices
in the dark, cruelty and fear
and rain on the windshield,
the blind curve, the stranger
up ahead.

The First Echo

For there was no echo
in the garden, for the trees
and the fruit of the trees
and their dense and many
leaves, and in this absence
they knew themselves to be
alone in the garden,
to be alone perfectly
together, but for the great
voice that seemed sometimes
to fill the spaces in
the vegetation and stilled all
the animals in the trees
and those that crept
along the ground, the voice
that did not echo
but seemed more
to saturate the very air.
It was only after,
in that after meant to be
life as we know it,
that he, walking behind her—
she was, and can't we
understand this, angry
with him—called out
to her about the high cliff
they were approaching,
which appeared to mark
the end of the traversable
landscape, and a moment later
heard a voice return: someone
was calling, the voice distant
and fading, calling *stop* saying
please saying *please come back.*

Oh, yes, he seemed to say

—Virginia Woolf

Just now the woman at the next
table said *I know that God
has called on me to leave
but I have not left
I have not looked to leave*
and isn't that the problem

with dying *I have not looked
to leave* your face said
beneath the first row of staples
planted in the field of your bruised scalp

and you spoke upon waking
in a tongue that was beautifully addled
as though you would lay down altogether

the burdens of language
and speak the clear speech
of the living soul

as though you had heard
God's blue voice in your ear
and said *wait   just wait*

Outside Her Bedroom Window
She Hears Birds

She wants to talk of late
of how the birds at dusk
will sing and sing—of how
they will, inside the spruce
outside her window, trill
their valediction for
the day, and how that song
calls the stars down, and how
it brings the darkness to
the trees, and how it brings
the possum out to raid
the compost bin, and how,
now readying for bed,
she wants and wants and wants
to sing and singing bring
the whole night on, the stay
against what cannot stay
become an invocation.

Alphabet for Paul

Apologies for not writing more often,
But you are dead and I
Cannot find the time to keep up with you.
Don't you have better things to do, anyway?
Everything's better, they said when we were kids.
Families are reunited.
God touches your dead dog and
He comes back to life. (The dog,
I mean.)
Just wait! Rest easy in the
Knowledge that life begins after
Life. Dead is the new 40.
My god, Paul, I'm sorry,
Never mind, what I'm trying to say is
One day you were here, you were
Present and accounted for, and then, in the
Quick of the brain, the tumor
Ripened like a fruit, and they opened and shut your
Skull like a
Trash can lid—
Until you
Vacated the premises,
Walked your own plank,
Xed out your eyes and left us all like
You meant to, left all of us
Zeroes, empty inside and out.

Earth vs. the Flying Saucers (1956)

When finally the hero, Dr. Russell Marvin, buries
his new wife's feet in Florida sand, it means God
bless America and young handsome love
and untrammeled stretches of honeymoon beach.
And there, in the glow from the screen
of the Montrose Theater, is my father. It's 1956,
he's 14, let out of chores for the evening
and driven to town, hair combed but still
smelling of barn. He feels a flutter as Carol
Marvin leans into her husband's chest. He presses
his fists deeper into his coat pockets. The next
morning, tending the cows, he remembers
the sky above the wreck of the Capitol dome
after the last wobbling, shrieking saucer
went down: just a blue sky, clouds
shredded like cotton and fading—nothing
descending to destroy us or steal us away.

Watching *The Blob* (1958) in the Days after the Movie Theater Shootings in Aurora, Colorado

When the blob, already swelled with townsfolk
subsumed in the quiet parlors of their homes, oozed
into the projection booth in the little downtown
movie house, the projectionist's screams were masked
by the recorded terrors of the movie villain's victims.
The theater was full of teens on dates, happy to be scared
together in the hot dark. The blob was red, of course,
as all our fears were then—a shapeless, faceless,
insidious force that could find us no matter where
we hid. It was the foreign red, and its only worthy
adversary was a teenaged—angry, mistrusted, in love
above his station—Steve McQueen. In other words,
America. Teenagers streamed screaming from the theater,
awakened from their cathartic dream of sex and fear
as the blob dropped from the booth's window, growing
larger by the moment, absorbing the lesser players
in the theater's back row. In the street, the crowd
accumulated to count its number. Of the blob,
McQueen knew only this: it can't be killed.

On a Pond at the Edge of the Wood

my father laughed at my mother
for saying so but my mother insisted
there off the curve of the road is the pond
and it's bottomless   bottomless my father
said confident as a parson it cannot be

bottomless if a pond goes down it can't
be forever   I was told I was told
said my mother of the rattling car
of bumptious teens careening drinking
it was said they were drinking

who missed the curve and sank
into the pond forever   they are still
sinking they are damned to fall
forever through its deepening
the father of one even swam its lengths

and found no trace of them   to which
my father said brown water said snapping
turtle pickerel tooth said braided knot of
water grass around the throat the rattling
car giving off a bloom of oil first

and later rust   no   no bottomless
my mother said bottomless like the heart
of winter like the love of god and in
the back seat having long given up
on the hole dug to China nonetheless

I dreamed the pond bottomless   dreamed
myself swimming down and down in my chest
the breath tightening like a rope pulled
to raise a child fallen in a well

Bird Light

we are not
my tribe the types
to see a soul up there

but this morning
my daughter found
to the west the sky's

sole opening
filled with light as
the morning

sun angled just
so above the clouds
and look she said

it is bird light the birds
are flying there
and singing making

light come through
and this I knew
was not a failure

of logic but its
grand success because
how beautiful

a world where
birdsong lights
the morning

in the western sky
oh to be lit
by bird light

to bathe in it
to sing the way
birds do

with their whole
bodies their whole
bodies the instrument

of song and if light
will come through
to let it

For Maria, Fifteen Days

This morning, crowning
the butter-headed daffodils,
a fat spring snow.

The arms of the cedar droop
in something approximating patience.
Snow collects

on the pink spines of the rose bush,
obscures the woodchuck's just-cut path.
Inside, a warm blanket

of silence settles around us,
a double to the snow—
even the dogs abide it.

Two weeks and one day
old, you stir at your mother's shoulder,
awakened by the pinch

of one of your simple needs.
Which one
is ours to determine.

I would like to bring you
to the window, show you the snow
as it deepens, say *look*

as the cowbird tilts
among the earliest buds of the oak.
You've settled again,

your face not a mask of peace
but peace clear down, peace as the snow
is the hand of peace

on the incipient
riot of spring, saying everything
in its time.

EVERY NEST
TO ASH

Witness to Murder (1954)

What has Barbara Stanwyck done
to deserve this, what but linger at her curtains

before closing them, as any single
woman might in 1954, in Los Angeles,

as any female interior
decorator might, any mistress of

interiors, lingering with the drapes
between her fingers long enough

to accidentally see George Sanders
in the opposite apartment

choke a woman till she dies.
What has she done

to deserve the cruel attentions
of Sanders' secretly unrepentant

former Nazi, who tries to prove her
merely hysterical, addled by dreams,

or the attentions of the cop
who names her to Sanders

as the witness ("the girl
across the street thought she saw you . . .")

then takes her to dinner. Or the attentions
of the psychiatrist at the state hospital

with glasses like the portholes
in a submarine, who grills her

in the long, cross-cut shadows of his
nearly empty office. What has she done

to earn men like these but not need them?
Only when, menaced on a high roof, screaming

as Sanders closes in, she falls
to a rickety platform just below the ledge

and lies perfectly still
in a perfect pile of womanhood—

only then has she earned the right
to be lifted, drawn up by one slender wrist

by the cop who sent the Nazi down
the elevator shaft, the cop

who loved her all along.

The Cops

Last night I dreamed I was arrested
for driving drunk. The dream ended
with me in tears, not about my punishment—
the night in jail, the court date, the long
bus to work—but about the maddening
indecision of the cops, here played by
distant friends, who weren't sure
whether or not they had a case. (*Tear
it up,* one whispered of the handwritten
report between them on the front seat,
as the other called his supervisor.)
In the dream, you were waiting for me—
I had just gone out to move the car—
and would soon begin to worry.
Surely, the cops in the front seat
were me, as figures in dreams must
always be: one careful of the rules,
the other of the anxious captive, and
neither sure what justice means.

Halloween

It never felt like me
egging the neighbor's LTD

or shoveling dog shit
into a bag and lighting it

on someone's porch. I felt
like someone else: immune to guilt,

cooler, stronger, braver,
the sort of boy who thrives on danger.

The plastic mask my face
wore rattled as I ran, the space

behind it breathy hot,
the eyeholes dark like streetlamps shot

with BB guns. The town
cop creeping with his floodlight down

the backstreets wouldn't know
who'd soaped the principal's car windows—

this hidden sycophant,
obsequious in class, pliant

for his parents. The one
voted most likely to be no fun.

Watch out! It's Halloween.
I'll smash your squash to smithereens.

Two Stories Up

When my neighbor crossed the street to me
where I held the baby in the front yard
we were watching the pigeons rearrange themselves
on the electric wire overhead and said to me
that the night before he had carried his handgun
up and down the street after someone had seen
a dark man in his driveway I knew Paul
that the world is so full of holes
we can never fill them all even
the windows we leave open some nights
in the bedroom where we sleep
facing the street are holes and the bullets
from my neighbor's pistol would not
fill them he thought the prowler
wanted into his truck which is silver
and huge and which the baby has taken to
demanding to see each day when it roars itself
awake like a dragon she says *see what's
the truck* and I lift her and carry her
to the window and we look at its massive
gleaming body as it rumbles and thrums
and didn't you once Paul get by stealing
car stereos when you were just
out of the army and living in your own
car your first son already out of
your life and you slept in your coat
as a stray beam of sodium light
hit the wires of the stereos you'd half-
hidden with laundry Paul my neighbor
said this man fled the scene he said *fled
the scene* through my backyard and now
each night I check three times each lock
and each window even the ones
two stories up and I place the heavy
metal flashlight weighted with its D-cell

batteries by the bed because everything
I love is in that house and I won't let it be
entered by someone who doesn't know
whether or not he is loved

Trap

It was the blunt face of the hatchet, the hammer
face, my father swung
against the forehead of the trapped raccoon.
I had laid the trap along the stream,
had nestled it in leaves where mud had showed
the coons were fishing.
It was two-hand work, that killing: at the first
blow, the coon pulled back, but slowly,
as though waking from a heavy sleep.
At the second, the trap chain pulled tight
against its stake, the stake that I had cut down
with that very hatchet.
You still could see
the shavings on the ground.
Both the coon's front paws
were caught. Have you ever studied
the paws of a raccoon? Have you seen their prints
at the fresh edges of a pond? They look
like hands, and they are sensitive enough
to tell by feel a crayfish from a rock.
My father swung the hatchet, three then four,
and the coon shivered and lay down. I had a choice
to pull away or stand
and watch. I stayed.

Early Self-Portrait as the Wolf Man (1941)

The wolf man knows what all sons know
upon spying the shopkeeper's daughter
through a telescope: that what a father insists
is a phase, a sickness, something to be got
hold of, is a gypsy curse. Stricken,
he grips the bedroom armchair—
the wolf-hair furs his legs and chest.
His voice distorts into a growl, a howl.
Deep in the fog-draped swamp, his animal
body drags him through the shadows
just beyond the pack of righteous men
turned out to save the town. The gypsy
horses startle at his scent. The woods are full
of traps, and he would step in every one.

Love in the Style of Harrison Ford

We wanted to be loved
in the presence of snakes.

We wanted someone
we could save.

We wanted to be loved so much
that we could walk away

from the woman
with I love you on her eyes.

We wanted to be almost bored
by close escapes,

by fights we won,
by turncoats turned

up dead. We wanted
to take one in

the shoulder, to be nursed
back to health

by a woman who,
dipping a cloth

into a basin of cool
water, would be moved

to say she loved us,
always had. Those

were the words that would
do it, and the next thing

you'd see we'd be back,
leather hat and whip

supple with oil, revolver
sparking in our hands,

bellowing her name
as she is taken from us

by some sneering evil,
giving us a reason to go on.

The Big Machines

We must have been 14
and walking in waders
the cindered berm and
carrying our fishing poles
from one stocked stretch
of the stream to another
and finding it hilarious
to wave grandiosely
at every passing car
until the pickup truck
that slowed as if under
the weight of its bad
intentions slowed
enough that we could see
its occupants and know them
from the terrors of the tech
wing of the junior-
senior high school where
the bored shop teacher
in his safety goggles
showed us how
to build a three-tiered
shelf and keep our thumbs—
these boys lived there
winding up their big
machines and passing
off (the story goes)
their pot plants
in the greenhouse
as tomatoes and what
did they want with us
as they pulled
to the margins of the county
road and threw the truck
into reverse so that its tail

lights glowered through
the fog of the exhaust
as though considering
our fate we fawns
caught out in suddenly
a wilderness

Sestina for Men

You're a man.
You can change a flat tire
along a dark and crowded highway without feeling
even a little
fear. You can fix
the broken washer. You know

not to admit what you don't know
because that is what a man
does, or doesn't, rather. Instead, you fix
yourself to facts. If your wife tires
of your act, it doesn't matter, even a little.
Even when she says you hurt her feelings,

that you have no feelings
to be hurt. You know
better. When you were little,
every man
you knew hid his bald spot, his spare tire,
lingered in the bathroom fixing

his tie. You know there is no fix
for some things, once they come apart. Feelings?
Well, I'm tired,
hungry sometimes. You know
what I'm saying. A man
shouldn't make a big deal out of something little.

And when a little
boy cries, his eyes fixed
on the playground's asphalt, the other boys sneer *woman*
because this boy, like a woman, makes the other boys feel
frightened. Of course, they don't know
it. They would tell you, if you asked them, that they're tired

of this boy and all his crying, tired
of having to stay in from recess because this little
girl got dirt on his dress. You know
how boys are. They'll fix
you good, until you're feeling
like a man.

In a Lonely Place (1950)

he is the cudgel
he beats the world with

Just now a goose

glided past my window and I
did not see it but could track its honk
from south to north as it came in
for its landing this is the season
of geese we often have to stop for
them as in their swaying walk
they lead their goslings from one
side of the street to the other why
did the goose cross the road I don't
know but if you get in its way it will
attack your knees and behind
the coffee shop a goose has claimed
as its own territory the small expanse
of blacktop where the trash cans wait
to be filled with coffee grounds
and the teenagers who work there
refuse to take the trash out until night
falls and the goose is sleeping
Pythagorus among other more lasting
theories believed in the transmigration
of souls because he said he heard
the voice of his dead friend
in the bark of a dog on the street
and so believed a soul might leap
at the moment of death from one body
to another nearby body I know
your soul is not in a goose chasing
teenagers behind a closed café though
you might do it just for the laugh or
because you want them to stop
and see you for a moment didn't you
always want so badly to be loved and what

can a man do when he is dying
to be loved but chase
from his hot and stinking turf
anyone approaching

Postcards

On one, a man in chaps and spurs
rides a giant grasshopper,

and here, a hapless family—
it seems somehow they do not see

their danger—smiles in the shadow of
a barn-sized squirrel. Here's one to prove

the fishing's good on some remote
mosquito-choked lake. Look, the boat's

about to founder or capsize
beneath that yellow perch the size

of a beluga whale. Reverse
the card to see the sender's terse

but plaintive note: Dear X, wish you
were here. Love, Y. We know the true

measure of a distance by
what forms of love can span it. High

sentiment falls short. Odes and songs
that hymn devotion go too long.

From here, it seems your only hope's
to speak your love in jackalopes.

The South Pole of the Moon

Take what you know of cold.
Take what you know of the dark.

Take what you know of—
I was about to say

love. Start again.
Take what you know

of the far edge of anything—
the far, wild, desolate edge.

Here, among the craters:
Shackleton, Amundsen, Scott.

The lonesome men. Men
of the long night. Men

clubbing seals to bathe in their blood.
This is what you know of cold:

the desperate dark, the stars
circling like hawks. That you

sought this place. You left
a warm bed—you left

butter melting thick bread,
a hillside field of heather.

You left the setter
by the stove, the soft

singing in the adjacent
room. You left

on a ship. You sorted your
supplies—you were so careful

of your supplies—
and trained dogs and hired men

and left on a ship.
And then the wheeling polar sky,

the screeching of the gulls—
no one to hear

your confession, every man
bitten in cold,

your ship ice-locked,
your ship stacked and groaning

in ice. You shoulder your pack
and push on.

After you have died,
many years

after you have died,
they will name for you

a crater on the South Pole
of the Moon,

because you know
what it means to be cold.

Yellowjackets

He made his hands a fire—
a twisted brand of newsprint
soaked in kerosene and lit,
kerosene poured too
into the tunnels of the jackets' hives,
dug out beneath the stones—
and flowers of fire
burned at the yard's edge
until every stinging thing
had turned to paper,
every nest to ash.

Another Alphabet for Paul

Anticipation, Paul, is the
balm of
cowards.
Depressed by what changes they have not
effected, they soothe themselves with
fantasies of
God's full smile, His huge
hand opening around something
incredible—a
jet ski, a job that won't
kill you,
love. Take
me as one example.
Never have I waited more fervently
on some beneficence than now, when,
petering
quietly into middle age, so
restrained I might be mistaken for
statuary, I
think of your
ugly scalp, the river of bruise
vivid along the incision. Don't
worry at your early
exit, Paul.
Your death makes
zealots of us all.

The Family Album

If anyone ever said, "the past is what you make it,"
it was my grandmother, cropping with her huge shears
outsiders from the family album: my cousin's
college girlfriend, the Fresh Air kid
who stayed with us one summer, the aunt
who left my uncle for her hypnotist.
All that remains are the contours
of their absence, a photo's ragged edge
reminding us, sending the mind back
into that gap—*who stood there once?*
How did we know her? To what
separate life did she retreat?
We know we wouldn't recognize her
now, the way you might return
to an old vacation spot to find condos
blocking the view of the beach. Still,
you'd linger, picturing your younger self
running through the sea grass, suddenly
braver and more beautiful than you ever were.

WHAT YOU KNOW
YOU CAN'T OUTRUN

Another Way to Be Kind

Among the pyramids
of pears and tangerines
among the squared-off
grapefruits gleaming
in the produce section
of the grocery store
I watch one man
take another by
his shoulders and say
looking into his eyes and
with a solid quiet voice
Just off the highway
to Rochester Minnesota
twilight bounds softly
forth on the grass
and so on with
the Indian ponies
and the terror of living
and it seems to me
a kind of intercession
as when witnesses
to a traffic accident
link hands to pray
a thing to do
when helpless faced
with another's need
I wonder what
the first man saw
in the other's eyes
and then I remember
the story that Robert
Bly I think it was
would lock Wright
in a chicken coop
on the Bly farm

in Minnesota
so that Wright
would make poems
instead of drinking
and this may be
another way to be kind
to step between
the loved one and
himself even as
you know he can't
be saved and I could
see it as a kindness
to me too because
that poem saved me
once and I imagine
Wright and wouldn't
Bly have called him
Jimmy I imagine him
sober enough to feel
sick the tongue
that would kill him
dry in his mouth
smelling the scratch
and shit of the coop
as the eggs cool
on their straw beds
beginning to think
about breaking

Typhoon Coming On

From her hospital bed my mother wept into the phone
over our forebears, the Boston shipbuilders

whose business was the East Indies trade—slavery
in other words—and in my mind

I saw the Turner painting, *Slavers Throwing Overboard
the Dead and Dying—Typhoon Coming On*

with its blazing sky, the ship going down, the blood
in the mouths of the sharks, the brown hands

reaching out of the water, that brown
manacled leg stretching out of the water

about to go down and the whole thing a swirling
vortex of hell—those were my people, throwing overboard

the dead and dying, my people on the ship
being swallowed by the red sky and the rising

sea, the mouth of the sky opening around them, the sky
taking them into its mouth, and the blood

in the mouths of the sharks not theirs
and the bloody mouths of the sharks were a blessing—*they sang*

as they went under. And how to read the toss of the storm
as anything but justice, and how to read the red sky

as anything but God's clean rage—and yet
it isn't, no matter how much we want to read it there,

for God is not the weather, and the weather is not
God, and it cares not for good nor evil, and troubles

itself not with the acts of men, even these
acts, this trouble, these slavers my people:

and among my people too this woman now
not yet dying, now grieving our history, the blood

we still carry, as the virus sets fire to her
nerves, and the sun descends between the pines

outside her window, and if there is hope for us
it must be that we feel ourselves

close enough to dying that the grief may come
unfettered, close enough that we may realize

that we are brine and history and precious
little else.

The Wa Wa Wes

—for Roger Reeves

Roger Reeves, I am grateful to you
for being committed to being
as you put it one hot afternoon
in April unruly. Roger Reeves,
I think of you in South Jersey,
in 1988, just a boy, probably
running somewhere, probably pretending
to catch a pass from Ron Jaworski,
whom people used to call
the Polish Rifle, which always
sounds to me like an ugly joke
about World War II, as in: this gun
that cannot save you from
your tormentor is called
the Polish Rifle. That isn't
very funny. According to my
dictionary, a reeve is "the chief
magistrate of a district in
Anglo-Saxon England," which
I do not think you are. My name
is the word from which
the word *silly* comes. There.
It used to mean innocent and came
to mean naïve, which must say
something about the evolution
of our cynicism. What do I mean
when I say *our*? But look, Roger,
here is *reeve* as a verb, this time
from the Dutch: "to thread
(a rope or rod) through a ring
or other aperture, especially
in a block," as in: *the slave
was held by a rope reeved
to the auction block.* Or

instead of *reeved* say *rove,*
as in: *Karl.* As in: *the end*
of the world as we know it.
No. As in: *the world*
as we know it. But what
do I mean when I say *we*?
Roger, in 1988, someone
from my little timber town,
its tannery shut down, returned
with an hour cassette-taped
from a Philadelphia hip-hop station,
which we passed around like
contraband because we'd never
heard a thing like Public
Enemy before, like Kool Moe Dee,
whose "Wild Wild West"
someone had transcribed
onto the tape cover as
"Wa Wa Wes," because that's
how much we knew about
America, that we could scramble
the song's world to nonsense, even if
the song's world is a white
American fantasy of lawlessness.
And a couple years later the basketball
coach told a story about a black
family emerging from a stand of trees
into someone's yard where he was
attending a barbecue and it was,
he said, like they were emerging
from the jungle—and everyone
thought it was funny so I kind of
smiled and made a noise
in my throat, because I had that

luxury, and because that's what
you do when you don't belong
on the basketball team but
you're the tallest kid in the school
and the town cop stopped you once
to tell you you should try out,
which was the only reason
you had to fear him. And later
you just nod when somebody
tells you with a terrifying
confidence that *look, there are*
black people and there are—
to make the point that he
is not a racist, only
a discerning observer of human
behavior who is able to tell
the difference, though by what
measure he does not say—or *look,*
someone says, *I don't have any*
problem with them which, you
will learn decades later, is almost
exactly what J. W. Milam said
when describing to William
Bradford Huie in *Look* magazine
how he killed Emmett Till—
Roger, I don't know why
I'm telling you this. I want
to believe my people
were minding their own
foolish business on their New
England dirt farms while someone
who looked like you was reeved
to a block on the courthouse steps
in this city, but I suspect they were

not because whose business is
the bound slave if not my people's?
I am descended from Daughters
of the American Revolution on
both sides. And I think of our
daughters, and when I say *ours*
I mean yours, I mean mine,
and I think of seeing your face
that hot afternoon in April
break unruly with love for her—
oh let the revolution come
in all forms of love unruly
to save us, to save us,
and when I say *us* I mean
every damned one of us.

Sharing the Bed with the Baby
When You're Gone

She takes your full side
sideways, arrays her arms and legs
in starfish pose,

sleeps till 3 a.m. then wakes
and asks for a banana.
Falls back to sleep

with the chunk I give her
still in hand. I stay
awake. Asleep, she looks

even more like you. She turns
and turning kicks my side,
and I think of all those weeks

before I met her that she kept you up
tap-tapping you,
the vessel she was

sealed in, like Annie Taylor
in the froth and roil
at the bottom of Niagara,

waiting in the barrel
she called Queen
to be lifted out alive.

We Invite the Bees In

We let the milkweed grow
into the railing by the door
and the bees trouble the little
white star-flowers
with the singular obsessiveness
of the lower creatures
                            at the door
I have in hand my keys and
my bag and the baby's
and the baby and the door
stands before me doing its
one job which is to be
closed when we are not
here and now that I think
of it when we are here too to
keep the dog in and the bees
and heat or cold and snow
out and I remember once
waking before dawn to find
the front door swung open
and the cooled air drifting
in like a guest who doesn't
care whose party this is and
nothing was broken or
missing and no one was hiding
in the shadows I had just mis-done
the latch and by some trick
of gravity the door had opened
to nothing because nothing
comes in uninvited
                        I let
the milkweed grow because
the bees come and bees
the radio tells me are dying
vastly and quietly and now

men truck hives across California
to pollinate the almond trees
one week and the olive trees
the next I have never seen
an almond tree in blossom I
have never stood among an
olive grove and listened to
the bees at their labor I watch
them now their little fuzzed backs
as they work in the mouths
of the flowers and I think I would
advise them not to waste
their time not to bother with me
stopping here beside the door
with a baby who is tired of waiting
we have a song we sing
to make more bearable
the waiting no bees it is better
better to be bent in the
very hour of your dying
into the mouth of a flower
however small

Flutes and Throats

It is the bending of the wind
we cry to dance to the wind
trapped and tunneled in us
the singer makes his body
hollow the singer fills her
self with sound and I
could never sing because
I could not would not
make that cavity in me
come open would not
make that opening enough
to bend the air through—
and then I found behind
the stacked stone fence
scrub apple shaded
the shinbone of a cow
and raised it toward
the sky and saw where
marrow was now air
and light and knew
that singing is
our natural state

The Lost Dog

We awake in the night   to a screaming
and it is her   screaming it is coming from
right in between us   she is screaming at us
that the stuffed dog   she holds in one arm
is really in another room   and we say *no baby*
it is right here   and she insists that we left it
on the living room sofa   eventually we realize
it doesn't matter   that she's holding it to her
as she cries   *we are sorry* we say
that you are missing your doggie   *we are*
so sorry   *you miss him* and finally
she slumps back   with her little arm still
around the the stuffed dog's neck   and I am
blind like that too   I wake blind
my arms   full and grieving
the absence of just   what I'm holding

Inscription

Dear Paul last week at a poetry reading
on the second floor of a little restaurant I
thought of you I was having a whiskey
and sitting quietly facing the bar when
as the poet read slowly and with portent
and her face lit from below by a small lamp
a family stopped startled in the doorway a man
and a woman and two little girls by the gravity
of our silence and the slow portentous voice
of the poet who was reading poems of a bridled
and tactful eroticism
      they entered slowly
and took menus and the reading pretended
not to notice them and they pretended to be
invisible and I thought of the time that you
wrote me after I had told you that I had become
a poet you said *poetry is my favy too* and I
thought *favy* and that you would probably
not understand the poems I write and that I felt
then what still seems to me an appropriate shame
at my arrogance and wondered exactly whom
that judgment condemned
      but Paul I loved
those portentous poems with their bridled
eroticism and the silence in the room
was sincere and open when the younger of the girls
began scribbling on her placemat with a
borrowed pen her mother hissed at her to stop
the little rollerball sounded in the silence
like a dump truck on a gravel road the way
at night a mouse ascending the innards
of your electric range might sound like a hammer
bouncing on a tin roof but Paul I'm writing
to tell you that finally I understand
and I am sorry and I know now

that you would have understood perfectly
why that little girl wanted to spoil
the pure white of that placemat
why she wanted to hear
that pen make its music

Sparkler

Little switch
of packed
silver torch-
lit and night
blooms a hissing
yellow flower
of sparks we
score the dark
crowding in
with our faces
lit then shadowed
shadowed then
lit we parry
and spin
one hand in
the chemical
glow one hand
in darkness

Smokehouse

Built just by
a man between
two pines
and streaming
all day low
smoke to wrap
the pine's
thighs and I
a child watch
this little room
that seems
as though it's
breathing and I
can feel its heat
upon my face
as inside
a piece of
mortal flesh
becomes
transformed

Landscape with Crop Duster and Cary Grant

North by Northwest (1959)

Oh Roger Thornhill, baked to brown, the sun
is beating you into the dry brown fields—
you run from what you know you can't outrun.

The road is dirt, and you—gray suit, no gun—
are worried that your fate is newly sealed.
Oh Roger Thornhill, broiled brown in the sun.

Who's crop-dusting where there ain't no crops? Run,
Roger! Another plot has been revealed.
Run from what you know you can't outrun.

You look up from the stony ditch. You're stunned.
Roger, run: high above, the biplane wheels
around on you, dear Roger, browned by sun.

Oh Roger in the fields! So far from cun-
ing girls and three-drink Mad Ave handshake deals!
You run from what you know you can't outrun.

At this distance, you could be anyone
suddenly nowhere, fearful, exposed, feeling
the baking, (Poor Roger!) the burning sun—
and running from what you know you can't outrun.

Consoling the Ghost

I'm sorry: Angie left.
Your name, the one she took and kept

is gone now too, replaced
by his whose ruddy, pockmarked face

now smiles on her wall—
and when I look at your page, Paul,

I see your wedding photo:
Angie's white dress, pink face, your total

joy at being there
at all. You'd grown sufficient hair

to hide the scar along
your scalp, and on your face the long

smile of the not-yet-dead.
It's fixed there now, now that you're dead.

It seemed at first too cruel—
you, dead, still grinning like a fool,

while she unfriended you.
The day you married her, the blue

sea looked like sky, and I
was far away. Your mother cried

to see you on that beach
in your pink bowtie, the cancer's reach

seemingly too short.
Yours and Angie's was the sort

of love made perfect by
the specter of its brevity.

So you and Angie burned
(while the sickness in your brain returned)

like lightning-struck dry grass.
Afterward, she couldn't tell love from ash.

Despite Everything

On the radio, the velvet drone
of the public radio announcer
relating what we know: where
the latest bomb went off, who
killed whom and in what
grisly fashion, how the sea
returns the children that it
drowns. And then the story
of the coral bleached to death
by heat and now it seems too
by sunscreen, something in
the sunscreen that we wear
because we know the sun
would eat our skin. And she
with her orange slices
seems not to notice even
that it's on until the story
ends and instead of human
voices now the light
tones of the transition music
and the hosts are in the studio
drinking water from plastic
bottles and my daughter
slides from her chair, lifts
one arm, then the other, and
begins to dance. Later,
when we go outside,
we watch the bees busy
in the blossoms of the squash,
and I am grateful, I tell them,
that they returned this year,
and then I lift my head and see
that among the clover that has
claimed our yard again
she's dancing. No music

but her own this time,
or else this isn't about music
but about a secret, like
the dance the bees do
to lead the other bees
to the fields of flowers.

ACKNOWLEDGMENTS

I am grateful to the following journals, in whose pages some of these poems first appeared, at times in slightly different forms: *Bellingham Review:* "Feeling Good Night and She Is Love," "We Invite the Bees In"; *Boulevard:* "The First Echo," *december:* "The Lost Dog," "Outside Her Bedroom Window She Hears Birds"; *Diode:* "*Witness to Murder* (1954)," "*Earth vs. the Flying Saucers* (1956)"; *Florida Review:* "Postcards"; *Greensboro Review:* "Sharing the Bed with the Baby When You're Gone"; *Gulf Coast:* "On a Pond at the Edge of the Wood"; *New Letters:* "The Cops"; *Smartish Pace:* "Watching *The Blob* (1958) in the Days after the Movie Theater Shootings in Aurora, Colorado"; *Sou'wester:* "For Maria, Fifteen Days"; and *Tar River Poetry,* "Halloween."

Gratitude, too, to my sisters, brothers, and others in the art; to my colleagues at the University of Missouri–St. Louis; and to my energetic and talented students. You are my people. Gratitude to the UMSL College of Arts & Sciences for the research award that freed up time to do this work, and to the St. Louis Regional Arts Commission for its financial support. Gratitude to my family for their generosity and love. And, as always, gratitude to Sonia—for every page.

NOTES

The title of "*Oh, yes, he seemed to say*" comes from the final sentence of Virginia Woolf's "The Death of a Moth": "Oh, yes, he seemed to say, death is stronger than I am."

The title of "On a Pond at the Edge of the Wood" comes from W. H. Auden's "Musée des Beaux Arts."

The quoted passage in "Another Way to Be Kind" is the opening of James Wright's "A Blessing."

The quotation in "Typhoon Coming On" is from Robert Hayden's brilliant, haunting long poem "Middle Passage."

"The Wa Wa Wes": As Roger Reeves would tell you, Ron Jaworski was not the quarterback of the Philadelphia Eagles in 1988. History here requires Randall Cunningham, from whom, I suspect, Roger would have been much more excited to catch a pass. Apologies to Roger, to Mr. Cunningham, and to the Eagles.

The title of "Flutes and Throats" comes from Heather McHugh's "After Su Tung-P'o."

The title of "Despite Everything" is from Jack Gilbert's "A Brief for the Defense."

7017

CPSIA information can be obtained
at www.ICGtesting.com
Printed in the USA
LVHW031831140219
607572LV00002B/379/P

9 780807 169636